Written by Melissa C. Marsted • Illustrated by Cait Irwin
Designed by Aileen Aquino

Text and
Illustrations copyright ©2020
by Lucky Penny Publications, LLC. No part of this
publication may be reproduced, stored in a retrieval system,
or transmitted in any form or by any means, mechanical, photocopying,
recording, or otherwise without written permission from the publisher.

Cover and Book Design by Aileen Aquino

For inquiries or more information, email us at melissa@luckypennypress.com
or visit our website at www.luckypennypublications.com or
@luckypennypublications Instagram.

ISBN: 978-1-945243-08-0

"Go confidently in the direction of your dreams!
Live the life you've imagined."

—Henry David Thoreau

Welcome to
ACADIA NATIONAL PARK

Acadia National Park is the only national park in all of New England, which is a group of six states on the far east side of the United States.

Acadia National Park is located in Maine on the island of Mount Desert. In the park, there are many small mountains, freshwater ponds, evergreen forests, and sandy beaches with steep rocky cliffs. You will soon meet a baby chickadee named DeeDee as she begins her journey through Acadia during the four seasons: spring, summer, fall, and winter.

Time to meet DeeDee!

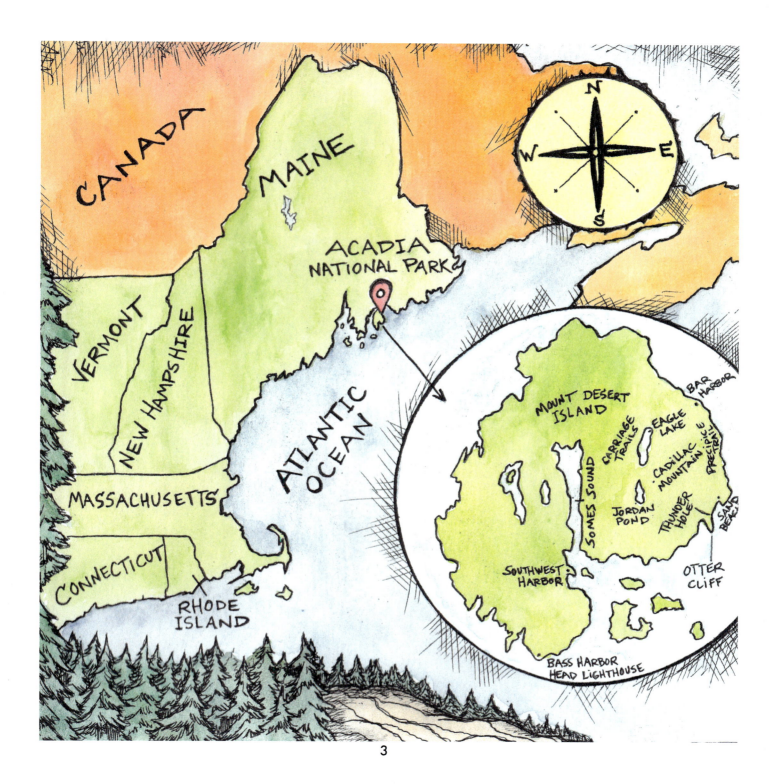

Well, hello there!

I'm DeeDee, a black-capped chickadee and a songbird. Listen for my call. Chickadee-dee-dee! Chickadee-dee-dee!

My momma found an abandoned woodpecker hole in this tree. She gathered moss and cozy rabbit fur to line her nest and laid six eggs. After twelve days of growing in our eggs, my siblings and I hatched. I was so squished inside the egg, and then I was really squished in the nest. My brothers and sisters just soared off, so now I have the nest all to myself.

But my momma said it's time for me to test my wings. I am scared!

Really scared!

"Come on, DeeDee. Take that hop and spread your wings. You will be in for a grand surprise. Follow me to this branch, and we'll decide where to fly from here.

"You have so many new friends to meet and so much to see. Trust your momma!

"One. Two. Three. Go!" MommaDee cheered.

"Ok, coming!"

"Yay! You did it!" MommaDee exclaimed. "Look over there, that's Eagle Lake. Let's take a quick flight and see who's there on this delightful spring morning.

"Head for those cattails near the shore. I see Mr. Blue Heron. He wants to teach you about determination and reaching for the stars.

"Fly there and say hello," MommaDee encouraged.

Chickadee-dee-dee!

"Well, good morning, little one. What's new with you?" asked Mr. Blue Heron.

"My momma is teaching me to use my wings so I can fly all around Mount Desert Island. I'm going to meet new friends and learn about the four seasons," I replied.

"I'm sure she told you that you were born in the spring. Then comes summer when the days will get much warmer and longer," Mr. Blue Heron said.

"Oh, yes! I was very chilly when I was first born and even colder after my brothers and sisters left the nest. I'm much warmer now, especially when I use my wings to fly!" I responded.

"Well, since you are exploring, fly over to Precipice Trail and see the beautiful views from up there," suggested Mr. Blue Heron. "It's a tough challenge, but you must believe in yourself!"

"Follow me up Precipice Trail! I'm going to take you to see some other adorable chicks. With spring coming to an end, summer is such a wonderful season when nature bursts alive," said MommaDee.

I flew with my momma up and up and up some more. I was so tired, but we finally made it to the top of the cliffs where we could see the peregrine falcons nesting.

"Look at those balls of puffy, white feathers! Let's not disturb them while they are getting morning treats from their parents. We'll head to Cadillac Mountain," said MommaDee.

"Is it far? My wings are aching," I complained as we leapt from the rocky cliff.

"We made it! This is the summit of Cadillac Mountain, the highest peak in all of Acadia National Park," my momma told me.

We arrived just in time for sunrise, too. Today is the summer solstice, which is the longest day of the year.

"Hello, Mr. Porcupine. Your quills might seem scary to your predators, but we know that you have a soft heart," I said.

"You must be rather tired and ready for your nap. You are nocturnal and like to play at night while the rest of us sleep. Now that it's daylight, it's time for you to sleep. Rest well, Mr. Porcupine!" I said as my momma and I began our flight to Sand Beach.

Look at all the shore birds! Those sandpipers and terns search for food at the water's edge. They eat whatever they can find in the sand like tiny insects, worms, and biofilm, which is a thin layer of yummy slime on the surface of the sand!

Soon, summer will come to an end. As fall begins, the days will get shorter and cooler. Some birds and other animals will start to migrate south to find warmer temperatures.

"I hear loud crashing. What is that?" I asked MommaDee.

"It's a perfect time to visit Thunder Hole," my momma responded.

Whoosh!

Wow! The waves from the Atlantic Ocean crash into the cave below and explode up the cliff walls in a forceful spew of water.

"The sprays of water feel great on this hot day!" I shouted with glee.

"Be careful, though," MommaDee warned.

After cooling off at Thunder Hole, my momma said, "We must be on our way. I want to introduce you to some cute mammals that play in the waves of the ocean. Then, we will continue to Jordan Pond where you can rest, and I will say good-bye."

We are so high above the ocean!

MommaDee said, "These are called Otter Cliffs. They are some of the highest cliffs along the east coast. Let's fly down to that landing so we can have a better look at that river otter pup playing in the water. His home is in the water. He doesn't mind how cold it is, even as the days get shorter. Otters are happy and curious little creatures that do well in all kinds of weather."

Look at him with that crab. He must be ready for lunch!

"DeeDee, you must be hungry, too. There's a special surprise waiting for us at Jordan Pond," my momma hinted.

So hungry!

"Here we are, DeeDee. I see a place to rest and taste some yummy treats! Jordan Pond Popovers!" MommaDee said.

"We can find some crumbs and sneak some bites when the people aren't looking! As we are getting closer to the winter season with its fluffy white surprise, the people will no longer be here to drop their crumbs. Always remember to eat berries from the bushes and insects hiding in the holes of trees," my momma taught me.

"Do you feel the air? It's getting cooler. The days will start getting shorter, and the leaves will change colors, too. Many of our friends with wings will start to migrate south. I will be leaving you soon, so you will have to find places to hide and keep warm while I look for a new hole to make a nest for next spring," my momma said.

"Well, hello, Miss Monarch. You must be getting ready to fly away, too. You have a very long journey to Mexico! The egrets and peregrine falcons will migrate, too, but not as far as all of the Monarch butterflies and the hummingbirds," said my momma as she waved to Miss Monarch.

"That plant is called milkweed. Baby monarch caterpillars eat the leaves before they transform into beautiful adult butterflies.

"The monarchs remind me that you, too, are transitioning from a baby chickadee into an adult. Remember to have the confidence to follow your own journey through Acadia National Park. I have been your guide, and now you will have to trust your way," MommaDee said.

"It is now the fall season, and today is the day for me to say good-bye, DeeDee.

"You have a few more stops to make before your year of adventure in Acadia National Park comes to an end.

"Beware of the bald eagles and snowy owls that might swoop down to get you. They can be very sneaky, so you must always pay attention," cautioned MommaDee.

"I have taught you what you need to survive and make your own way on Mount Desert Island."

"But I'm scared, Momma," I replied.

"DeeDee, you are strong. Have courage. Trust your senses.

"You are big now! I love you, my darling."

"Bye-bye, Momma."

Here I go! Off to explore the woods on my own. I know I can do this.

My momma told me about the Carriage Roads that have been here for many years and the moose that like to saunter through these paths.

"Hello, Mr. Moose. I hope you don't mind if I take a break on your antlers."

"I don't mind at all, little friend. Luckily, they are the perfect perch for you now, but they will soon fall off during the beginning of the winter season," Mr. Moose responded.

"Thank you, big buddy. A quick rest is exactly what I need before I fly, fly, and fly away!"

Chickadee-dee-dee!

My momma warned me to be very careful when I fly across Somes Sound. I want to explore as much of Acadia as I can, so I must cross this narrow channel of water to get to the land on the other side. I have to be quick to avoid the watchful eye of a bald eagle.

Uh-oh! I see him. He probably thinks he can get me. I'll head to those lobster traps on the other side of the sound.

I'm almost there!

Phew! That was close.

I made it to Southwest Harbor. The lobster fishermen are emptying their traps. They can fish for lobster all year long, even during the cold, short days of the winter months.

Here I can find safe places to hide from bald eagles and other predators. But the lobsters' two huge claws sure are scary. Snap, snap, snap!

I feel a winter chill in the air, and I miss my momma. There is still so much to see.

I can do this.

I know I can.

I'm going to head to Bass Harbor Head Lighthouse! It's the only lighthouse on all of Mount Desert Island. I'll have to be fast, since there is less daylight during the winter months.

I thought I was safe, but oh no! My momma warned me about Mr. Snowy Owl! "Watch out for his sharp talons," she said.

Luckily, I can see his white body perched in the evergreen trees, so I have time to escape.

"Be careful of the snowy owls when the white winter surprise comes," my momma told me. "They can camouflage and blend in, so they can be very hard to spot."

Wow! That was a tiring flight.

I found this peaceful setting next to the lighthouse to watch the sunset. Today is the winter solstice, which marks the shortest day and longest night of the entire year.

I love to gaze at the majestic colors in the sky, but I sure am ready for a good night of sleep before I finish my journey through Acadia National Park.

I smell something! I feel something! I can taste it, too!

It's fluffy, and it's white. This must be my grand surprise!

"DeeDee, it is!" exclaimed Ms. Blue Jay.

"It's snow! It's snow!" chirped Mr. Cardinal.

I can watch the snow from here. It's light. It's fluffy. It's peaceful and calming, and I am safe.

This is the end of my year of adventure in Acadia National Park. It was great to see all four seasons: spring, summer, fall, and now winter.

My wings are tired, so it's time for a little rest. Goodnight, my friends. See you in the morning!

Chickadee-dee-dee!

Wildlife Adventures for Young Readers

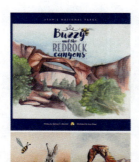

Buzzy and the Redrock Canyons
WRITTEN BY MELISSA C. MARSTED AND ILLUSTRATED BY IZZY GREER

Buzzy the bee zips across the state of Utah introducing readers to Utah's five national parks, starting with Arches, then continuing to Canyonlands, and finally crossing the state to Capitol Reef, Bryce Canyon, and Zion National Parks. Buzzy teaches readers about animals and endangered species that live in the parks as well as how arches, hoodoos, and spires were formed many years ago. *Buzzy and the Red Rock Canyons* is a great introduction to the wonders and magic of nature and the national parks system, originally established over 100 years ago.

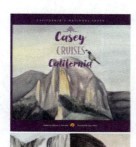

Casey Cruises California
WRITTEN BY MELISSA C. MARSTED AND ILLUSTRATED BY IZZY GREER

Readers join Casey, a California quail, on a journey through the nine national parks in his beautiful home state. Casey starts the adventure in the north at Redwoods National Park and narrates his way southward through forests with massive trees, majestic glacial formations, searing deserts, and sublime Pacific Islands, finally returning to the north to end Casey's travels at Pinnacles National Park, and the Golden Gate Bridge, the world's gateway to California. Along the way Casey meets a variety of animal friends who help him understand the unique qualities of each park, and he also teaches readers some of the history and amazing fun facts about the parks.

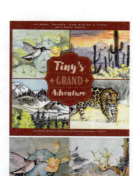

Tiny's Grand Adventure
WRITTEN BY MELISSA C. MARSTED AND ILLUSTRATED BY RUTHANNE HAMRICK

Join Tiny, a black-chinned hummingbird, as he travels across the American Southwest visiting seven national parks in Nevada, Arizona, New Mexico and Texas. Tiny meets many animal friends along the way; these friendships show us all that the differences between them are at the heart of the wonder of nature. It's a long journey for this little hummingbird, but as Tiny flies freely from place to place without borders or walls, he is proof positive that even the smallest of us can do big things.

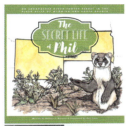

The Secret Life of Phil
WRITTEN BY MELISSA C. MARSTED AND ILLUSTRATED BY CAIT IRWIN

The Secret Life of Phil explores the Black Hills of Wyoming and South Dakota through the journey of an endangered black-footed ferret. Phil encounters other endangered species and hides from predators in awe-inspiring places like Badlands National Park, Devils Tower National Monument, and Mount Rushmore National Memorial. The black-footed ferret is protected by the Endangered Species Act. Our story aims to raise awareness among our readers about endangered species and the important role we all play in protecting them. Most of all, *The Secret Life of Phil* seeks to inspire a sense of wonder about the beauty and magic of nature.

Molly's Tale of the American Pikas
WRITTEN BY MELISSA C. MARSTED AND ILLUSTRATED BY RUTHANNE HAMRICK

Molly the Meadowlark takes readers on a journey through five national parks that are currently threatened by climate change. Molly introduces us to the pika, an adorable mammal that can be found in each of the national parks Molly visits. Molly teaches young readers about pikas, including how they escape from other animals who hunt them. But what is an even greater danger to our pikas than all of these predators? Read *Molly's Tale of the American Pikas* to learn more about how changes in weather and climate are one of the biggest threats to the pika's way of life.

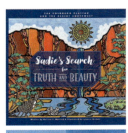

Sadie's Search for Truth and Beauty
WRITTEN BY MELISSA C. MARSTED AND ILLUSTRATED BY LYNETTE NICHOLS

Join Sadie, a greater sage-grouse, as she takes her three chicks throughout the Colorado Plateau and tells them stories about the ancient ruins and the magnificent rock formations that they encounter along the way. Sadie protects her chicks from the desert predators and teaches them how to search for water. On their journey, Sadie will reveal secrets to her chicks passed down by the Ancestral Puebloans. The chicks will learn survival skills. Will they find enough water to mature into adults? Open the pages filled with magical illustrations to learn more about the desert southwest.

About the Designer

Aileen Aquino graduated with a BS in Visual Communication Design from The Ohio State University. She has been working at various design firms, architectural firms, and contemporary art museums for close to 20 years. Aileen specializes in print design and, in her free time, creates pieces for her own letterpress company in Salt Lake City. She enjoys exploring the outdoors with her two children – whether it's skiing, hiking, mountain biking, or climbing – and reveling in their awe of the world around them. She is passionate about designing books she can share with her children, who have inherited her love of books, art, and travel.

photo credit:
Jamie Lewis

About the Illustrator

photo credit:
Julie Buckles

Cait Irwin is a professional artist as well as a published author, activist, entrepreneur, naturalist, and world traveler. Being an artist and having a deep connection with the natural world are two major constants in her life. Her artwork spans a wide spectrum of mediums, styles, and subject matter.

A native of South Dakota, Cait graduated from Northland College in Wisconsin in 2003 with a BA in Studio Art with an emphasis in environmental studies. She stayed in the Northwoods area for several years during which time she created murals, wrote a book, and taught herself woodworking. Cait eventually moved to Council Bluffs, Iowa to be closer to family and become a full-time artist. Six years ago, she founded Irwin Artworks, LLC.

To learn more about Cait, visit her website www.irwinartworks.com. Her artwork is also available for purchase at www.etsy.com/shop/irwinartworks.

About the Author

photo credit:
Eric Sullano

Melissa C. Marsted is the founder of Lucky Penny Publications which publishes children's books, memoirs, and non-fiction titles. She often consults with other authors seeking to publish their own books.

Melissa grew up in Connecticut as a competitive skier, runner, and swimmer. Since turning 50 years old and becoming an empty-nester, she has turned her attention to ultra-running and adventure sports including climbing and back-country skiing. While running her second 50k in November 2015, she came up with the idea to write children's books about the national parks. *DeeDee's Year of Adventure* is the seventh in the series, Wildlife Adventures for Young Readers. Through this series, she wishes to share her love of our national outdoor treasures and to advocate for the importance of saving our public lands and spending time in nature.

With a BA in Classical Greek from Harvard University and an MA in Organizational Management from Antioch University, Melissa worked in non-profit management for more than twenty years before starting Lucky Penny Publications in 2010. She is currently pursuing her MFA in Creative Writing with Pacific University while also writing the next book in the series and her running adventure memoir, *Finding Feathers*.

Melissa has two grown sons and lives in Park City, Utah, with her Jack Russell terrier, Aro and her recently inherited very fat cat, Twinkles.

Jordan Pond House Popover Recipe*

Prep Time: 15 mins / Cook Time: 30 mins / Total Time: 45 mins

Ingredients

2 large eggs at room temperature	1 cup sifted all-purpose flour	Speck of baking soda
1 cup whole milk	1/4 teaspoon salt	

Instructions

1. Preheat oven to 425°.
2. Sift and measure flour, salt and soda. Set aside.
3. Beat the eggs at high speed until lemon colored (2-3 minutes).
4. On slowest speed, beat very slowly and until well mixed 1/2 cup of the milk.
5. Add slowly (with mixer going on slow speed) the dry ingredients.
6. When mixed, stop beating.
7. Scrape sides of the bowl with a spatula.
8. Beat at medium speed and slowly add the remaining milk.
9. Beat 2 minutes.
10. Place well-greased muffin tin or popover pan into oven to warm up for five minutes.
11. Turn mixer to high speed and beat 5-7 minutes.
12. Batter should be smooth and about the thickness of heavy cream.
13. Pour batter through a strainer, and into well-greased, preheated muffin tins or popover pan.
14. Bake on the middle shelf of the preheated oven at 425° for the first 15 minutes.
15. Without opening the oven, reduce the temperature to 350° and bake 15 - 20 minutes longer.
16. Popovers are best served at once, but may be kept in the warm oven for up to five minutes.
17. Serve immediately with butter and strawberry jam. **Makes 6 servings.**

If you've ever visited Acadia National Park or plan a visit now that you have read this book, you will want to make sure you make reservations at the Jordan Pond House where they serve their famous popovers.

This recipe was borrowed from the blog: Through Her Looking Glass and authored by Allie Taylor.

Acadia National Park
Twelve Fun Facts

- The world's first national park, Yellowstone, was created in 1872 by President Ulysses S. Grant. During the period from 1872 to 1916, the United States gained 11 more national parks.

- Congress passed and President Woodrow Wilson signed the National Park Service Act establishing the national park system in 1916.

- As of April 2020, the National Park Service encompasses 62 national parks with an additional 357 national monuments, preserves, and historical sites covering roughly 85 million acres in all 50 states.

- California has the most national parks with nine, followed by Alaska with eight, Utah with five, and Colorado with four.

- Acadia National Park is the only national park in all of New England, which is comprised of six states – Connecticut, Massachusetts, Rhode Island, New Hampshire, Vermont, and Maine.

- Conservationist George Dorr devoted many years of his life to preserving Acadia and helped to acquire 6,000 acres by 1913. Dorr eventually offered the land to the federal government, and in 1916, President Wilson announced the creation of Sieur de Monts National Monument. Three years later, the area was renamed and established as Layafette National Park. In 1929, the name was changed again to Acadia National Park. It now protects and preserves over 47,000 acres.

- There are over 4,600 islands off the coast of Maine. Mount Desert Island, home to Acadia National Park, is the largest island off the coast of Maine, but it is the second largest island—after Long Island—along the entire east coast.

- Mount Katahdin is the highest peak in Maine at 5,267 feet. Cadillac Mountain on Mount Desert Island is only 1,527 feet, but it is the first place to see the sunrise in the United States.

- There are 13 species of otters including the river otter, which is the only species of otter found on the east coast of the United States.

- The chickadee was named the state bird of Maine in 1927.

- Chickadee's wings beat about 27 times per second. This compares to a hummingbird's 80 beats per second.

- The female chickadee will lay about six eggs that are white with speckles. She will incubate (sit on) them for about 12 days while the male brings her food.

For more information about Wildlife Adventures for Young Readers or Lucky Penny Publications, please email us at melissa@luckypennypress.com. For updates on our newest books, please click on our website www.luckypennypublications.com, our Instagram @luckypennypublications, or https://www.etsy.com/shop/findingfeathersgifts.

Made in the USA
Monee, IL
21 June 2023

36379634R00031